Sherlock Holmes:
The Top-Secret Plans

LEVEL ONE   400 HEADWORDS

OXFORD

UNIVERSITY PRESS

Great Clarendon Street, Oxford, OX2 6DP, United Kingdom

Oxford University Press is a department of the University of Oxford. It furthers the University's objective of excellence in research, scholarship, and education by publishing worldwide. Oxford is a registered trade mark of Oxford University Press in the UK and in certain other countries

This edition © Oxford University Press 2014

The moral rights of the author have been asserted

First published in 2014

2022

14

No unauthorized photocopying

ISBN: 978 0 19 424981 2   Book
ISBN: 978 0 19 463946 0   Book and Audio Pack

Printed in China

This book is printed on paper from certified and well-managed sources

ACKNOWLEDGEMENTS

Illustrations by: Giorgio Bacchin/Beehive Illustration.

The publisher would like to thank the following for their permission to reproduce photographs: Alamy p.25 (Regent Street, London, 1892/© The Print Collector); Bridgeman Art Library p.19 (Royal Arsenal, Woolwich/English Photographer, (20th century)/Private Collection/© Look and Learn/Peter Jackson Collection); iStockphoto p.38 (walking stick/arsela); Shutterstock pp.31 (vintage cash box/optimarc), 40 (London Underground/Tupungato), 41 (Paris Metro/Huang Zheng).

DOMINOES

Series Editors: Bill Bowler and Sue Parminter

Sherlock Holmes: The Top-Secret Plans

Sir Arthur Conan Doyle

Text adaptation by Jeremy Page

Illustrated by Giorgio Bacchin

Sir Arthur Conan Doyle (1859-1930), born in Edinburgh, Scotland, is best known as the creator of Sherlock Holmes. He started writing after working as a doctor, and soon became one of the world's best-known authors. *Sherlock Holmes: The Blue Diamond*, *The Emerald Crown*, *The Norwood Mystery* and *The Sign of Four* are also available as Dominoes. His adventure story *The Lost World* is also a Domino title.

OXFORD
UNIVERSITY PRESS

BEFORE READING

1 Here are some of the people in *The Top-Secret Plans*. Who are the bad people in the story? What do you think?

| **1** Sherlock Holmes | **2** Doctor Watson | **3** Mycroft Holmes | **4** Colonel Valentine Walter | **5** Lestrade of Scotland Yard |

| **6** Arthur Cadogan | **7** Violet Cadogan | **8** Sidney Johnson | **9** Hugo Oberstein | **10** Mason |

2 Are these sentences true or false? What do you think?

		True	False
a	Sherlock Holmes is a famous detective.	☐	☐
b	Mycroft is Sherlock's brother.	☐	☐
c	Colonel Walter is Mycroft's good friend.	☐	☐
d	Watson is Sherlock's doctor.	☐	☐
e	Lestrade lives with Watson.	☐	☐
f	Arthur Cadogan works in an army office.	☐	☐
g	Violet is Arthur's sister.	☐	☐
h	Johnson works with Arthur Cadogan.	☐	☐
i	Oberstein is British.	☐	☐
j	Mason finds a dead body.	☐	☐

1. A Visit from Mycroft

It was a dark autumn morning in 1895. My friend Sherlock Holmes, the famous detective, and I, Dr Watson, were in the **sitting room** of our house in Baker Street in London when a **telegram** arrived. Holmes opened it at once, and laughed. I looked quickly across the room at him.

'Why are you laughing, Holmes?' I asked.

Holmes looked back at me with his cold, blue eyes.

'Because this telegram is from my brother Mycroft,' he said. 'He wants to speak to me at once about Mr Arthur **Cadogan**. Do you know this man, Watson?'

'I saw something about him in today's **newspaper**. But now I can't remember the story,' I answered.

'And my brother Mycroft – what do you remember about him?' asked Holmes with a smile.

'Not much,' I answered. 'I met him once – long ago. Tell me more about him.'

sitting room a room in a house where people sit and talk

telegram a very short letter that arrives very quickly

Cadogan /kəˈdʌgən/

newspaper people read about things that happen every day in this. *The Times* is a famous newspaper.

1

'He's a very **clever** and important man. He works for the **government**. He knows everything about everything. So why does he want to speak to me? Why does he want to visit our home in Baker Street? And who is Mr Cadogan?'

I opened *The Times* and looked for the story.

'Here it is!' I cried suddenly. 'A worker found Cadogan's dead body near Aldgate Station on the London **Underground** on Tuesday morning.'

'Tell me more, Watson,' said Holmes.

I began to read the story in *The Times* to him. 'The dead man was Mr Arthur Cadogan. He was twenty-seven years old. He lived with his wife, Violet, in **Woolwich** and he worked at Woolwich **Arsenal**.'

'Now I understand!' cried Holmes. 'Mycroft is interested because Cadogan worked for the government!'

'On Monday night,' I said, 'Cadogan was in Woolwich with his wife. They had tickets for the **theatre**. Suddenly he left her in the street. But why? She doesn't know. At six o'clock the next morning, a worker found his dead body.'

'Near Aldgate Station,' said Holmes. 'I see. And was Cadogan badly **injured**?'

'Yes, he was.'

'Then he **fell** from the train – or somebody **pushed** him.

Perhaps he was dead before they pushed him out. Tell me more, Watson.'

'Cadogan's train came from West London, but where did he get on? The **police** don't know,' I said. 'There was no train ticket in his pockets, only some money, two theatre tickets – and some **papers**.'

'Very interesting,' said Holmes. 'How did he get on the train without a ticket? Perhaps somebody took it. But why?' Holmes stopped and thought. 'Hmm. Cadogan worked for the government at Woolwich Arsenal, he had some important papers, and my brother Mycroft is interested in this. And so, Watson, I am interested, too. Now, where is Mycroft?'

Minutes later, Mycroft Holmes arrived at our door. He was a tall, fat man with a very clever face. With him was our old friend Lestrade, the Scotland Yard detective. Mycroft took off his coat and sat down.

'This is very bad, Sherlock,' he said. 'The government isn't happy. Do you know the story?'

'Watson read it to me from *The Times*,' answered Sherlock. 'What were the papers in Cadogan's pocket?'

'They were **plans** for a new British **submarine** – the Bruce-Partington submarine. They're **top-secret**, and must always stay in a **safe** at Woolwich Arsenal.'

'Then why were they in the pocket of a dead man near Aldgate Station?' asked Sherlock.

'We can't understand it, Mr Holmes,' said Lestrade.

'And it's worse than that,' said Mycroft. 'There were ten papers in the safe at Woolwich. But we only found seven papers in Cadogan's pocket. The three most important papers weren't there. Where are they? We don't know!'

police they look for people who break the law

paper something with important writing on it; you write on this

plan something that you write or draw before you make something later

submarine a ship that goes under the water

top-secret that the government doesn't want people to know about

safe a box that people put important things in so thieves can't get them

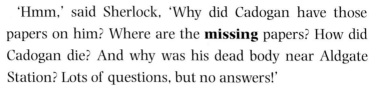

missing not there

responsible when you must be careful about something, and when things go wrong, it's because you aren't doing this well

key you can close or open a door with this

'Hmm,' said Sherlock, 'Why did Cadogan have those papers on him? Where are the **missing** papers? How did Cadogan die? And why was his dead body near Aldgate Station? Lots of questions, but no answers!'

'And so we need *you*, Sherlock,' said Mycroft.

Sherlock looked at his brother, and at the police detective. 'Tell me more,' he said.

Mycroft smiled, and answered. 'Sir James Walter is **responsible** for all the papers at Woolwich Arsenal. He's a good man. Most importantly, he has one of the two **keys** to the safe. The plans were there when he left Woolwich at three o'clock on Monday afternoon for London. He took his key with him.'

'Why did he go to London?' asked Sherlock.

'He needed to meet someone from the government. He left the man's London home late that night.'

Sir James Walter

'Right. So Sir James didn't help Cadogan take the plans,' said Sherlock. 'Who has the *second* key to the safe?'

'Mr Sidney Johnson,' answered Mycroft. 'He's forty years old. He lives near Woolwich Arsenal with his wife and five children. He first worked for the government when he was a very young man. He doesn't talk much, and people don't like him, but he's a good worker.'

'And where was Sidney Johnson on Monday evening?' asked Sherlock.

'At home with his wife all evening, he says. And he had his key with him,' Lestrade answered.

'Tell me about Cadogan,' Sherlock said.

'He began working at Woolwich Arsenal ten years ago,' said Mycroft. 'He worked with the plans. Johnson didn't.'

Sidney Johnson

'So Cadogan took the plans from the safe,' said Sherlock. 'Perhaps he wanted to **sell** them to someone. But how did he get the key to the safe?'

'And the key to the room, and the key to Woolwich Arsenal, too!' said Mycroft. 'We don't know.'

'So what do we know?' asked Sherlock. 'First: Cadogan left his wife in the street in Woolwich. Second: he didn't go to the theatre that night. Third: he went to London with the plans. And fourth: he died, perhaps near Aldgate Station. Did he sell the plans in London? Then why did he finish in Aldgate, and not back in Woolwich?'

'He wanted to sell the plans but he wanted lots of money for them, we think,' said Lestrade. 'There was a **fight** over the money, and Cadogan died. Then his killer took the three most important papers from his pocket.'

'But then why did Cadogan have tickets for the theatre that night, and no underground train ticket?' cried Mycroft. 'Sherlock, can you help us?'

Sherlock looked at his brother for some time.

'Yes, I can,' he said in the end, and stood up. 'This is all most interesting. And now I must find some answers to all those questions. Come, Watson.'

sell *(past* **sold***)* to take money for something

fight when someone hits people again and again

5

READING CHECK

Choose the right words to finish the sentences.

a Holmes laughs because a telegram arrives from…
1 Arthur Cadogan. ☐
2 his brother. ☑
3 Lestrade. ☐

b Watson met Mycroft…
1 many times before. ☐
2 a week ago. ☐
3 a long time ago. ☐

c Arthur Cadogan lived…
1 with his wife in Woolwich. ☐
2 at Woolwich Arsenal. ☐
3 with his wife in Baker Street. ☐

d An Underground worker found Cadogan's body…
1 in West London. ☐
2 near Woolwich Station. ☐
3 near Aldgate Station. ☐

e In Cadogan's pocket there were…
1 all the top-secret plans. ☐
2 some of the top-secret plans. ☐
3 two train tickets. ☐

ACTIVITIES

WORD WORK

Find new words in Chapter 1 to complete these sentences.

a Holmes and Watson are in their **s**.itting .room..... when Mycroft and Lestrade arrive.

b Watson reads about Arthur Cadogan in the **n**......................... .

c Lestrade works for the London **p**......................... .

d Holmes and Mycroft are two very **c**.........................men.

e Mycroft works for the British **g**......................... .

f Sir James Walter is **r**.........................for the top-secret plans.

g They usually stay in a **s**.........................in Woolwich Arsenal.

h You cannot open this without a **k**......................... .

i The plans are for a new British **s**......................... .

j Did Cadogan die in a **f**.........................with someone?

k Did someone **p**.........................him from a train?

l Was he was badly **i**.........................when he fell?

m Cadogan had two **t**.........................tickets on him.

n Where are the **m**.........................papers now?

o Did Cadogan want to **s**.........................the plans to someone?

GUESS WHAT

What happens in the next chapter? Write *Holmes*, *Watson*, *Mycroft*, or *Lestrade* in each space.

a ...., ...and , ...go to Aldgate Station.

b ....writes a telegram to................. .

c ....buys two train tickets.

d ....and.................go to Woolwich.

e ....wants to speak to Sir James Walter.

7

2. The Body on the Railway Line

An hour later, I stood by a **railway line** near Aldgate Station with Sherlock Holmes and Lestrade. Underground trains came out of their **tunnels** near Aldgate, and the railway lines there were open to the sky.

An old station worker with a red face spoke to us. 'My name's Mason,' he said slowly and carefully. 'And I found the young man's body here. He fell out of a train at about midnight on Monday, we think.'

'Was there a fight on a train on Monday?' asked Holmes.

'No,' answered Mason. 'We don't know of any fights. And we never found the young man's train ticket. There were only theatre tickets in his pocket.'

'Did you find any of the trains with an open door?' Holmes asked.

'No,' said Mason.

railway line a train moves on this

tunnel a long hole that underground trains go through

'We learned something interesting this morning,' said Lestrade. 'Someone in a train from West London heard a noise just before the train came into Aldgate Station. Perhaps it was the noise of Cadogan's dead body when it fell.'

8

'Perhaps,' said Holmes. 'But what are those things over there, Mr Mason?'

'Those are **points**, Mr Holmes,' answered Mason. 'Many different railway lines meet here, you see.'

Suddenly Holmes was very excited.

'Ah, and when trains go over points, they change **direction**! Hmm. Very interesting. Now, was there any **blood** on the railway line under the body when you found it? I don't see any now.'

'No, Mr Holmes, there wasn't,' said Mason.

'But Cadogan was badly injured, we know, so why was there no blood? What do you think, Watson?'

I am a doctor, but I had no answer for my friend.

'Now I'm very interested, Watson. Come. We must go to Woolwich. Goodbye, Lestrade. And thank you for your help, Mr Mason,' said Holmes.

He walked away, and I went after him. Lestrade began to say something, but then stopped. He wasn't happy.

points railway lines have these; you move them right or left so that a train can go onto a different line

direction where something is going

blood this is red; you can see it when you cut your hand

We took a train to London Bridge station. Holmes stopped there, and wrote a telegram to his brother.

> MYCROFT,
>
> I'M BEGINNING TO UNDERSTAND MORE.
>
> PLEASE SEND ME THE NAMES AND **ADDRESSES** OF ALL **FOREIGN AGENTS** NOW IN BRITAIN.
>
> SHERLOCK

'I need those names, Watson,' said Holmes. 'With them, we can understand more.'

I looked at my friend's face. He was now very excited.

'So why did Cadogan die?' I asked him.

'Why? – I don't know!' answered Holmes, 'But I know something about *how* he died. He didn't die near Aldgate Station, I know that. He fell from the **roof** of the train when it moved over those points and changed direction. There was no blood from his body on the railway line because he didn't die there. We must learn what happened in London on Monday night.'

'So what do we do next, Holmes?' I asked my friend.

'First we need two tickets to Woolwich,' he said. 'Cadogan had no ticket for his **journey** because he was dead when he began it. But you and I need tickets.'

I brought our tickets back from the ticket office.

'There's a train to Woolwich in ten minutes,' said Holmes.

We found our train and got on it. My friend closed his eyes and thought. I looked out of the window at the station. I thought about Cadogan. He came to London from Woolwich on Monday night, and never went home again. Then I thought about his wife, Violet. She wanted

address the number and the street where somebody lives

foreign agent somebody who works secretly in one country for the government of a different country

roof the top of a train

journey when you go far

to go to the theatre with her husband that evening, and never saw him again. Suddenly I felt very angry. 'We must find Cadogan's killer, Holmes!' I cried. 'We must do it for his wife.'

Holmes looked at me with his cold, blue eyes, but said nothing. Then he closed his eyes again.

After some minutes, our train left London Bridge Station. How much did my friend truly understand about Cadogan's **death**?

At Woolwich Station, we got off, and waited for a **cab**.

'Where are we going now, Holmes?' I asked.

'We need to visit many people,' he answered, 'but first we must go to the house of Sir James Walter. He's responsible for the submarine plans – or *was* responsible for them before all this happened! He's a good and important man, my brother tells us. So we must begin with him.'

Holmes looked at his watch. 'We can't wait any longer,' he said. 'I need to talk to Sir James now. Come, Watson!'

We walked from the station to Sir James's house.

death when someone stops living

cab a taxi

READING CHECK

Put these sentences in the correct order. Number them 1–7.

a Holmes and Watson leave Lestrade at Aldgate. ☐

b Holmes writes a telegram to his brother, Mycroft. ☐

c Holmes and Watson walk to Sir James Walter's house. ☐

d Holmes and Watson wait for a taxi at Woolwich Station. ☐

e Holmes questions Mason near Aldgate Station. ☐ 1

f Holmes and Watson take a train to London Bridge. ☐

g Holmes and Watson go by train to Woolwich. ☐

WORD WORK

1 Find new words from Chapter 2 in the letter square.

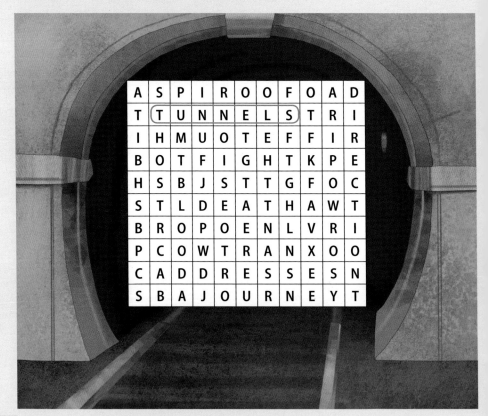

A	S	P	I	R	O	O	F	O	A	D
T	T	U	N	N	E	L	S	T	R	I
I	H	M	U	O	T	E	F	F	I	R
B	O	T	F	I	G	H	T	K	P	E
H	S	B	J	S	T	T	G	F	O	C
S	T	L	D	E	A	T	H	A	W	T
B	R	O	P	O	E	N	L	V	R	I
P	C	O	W	T	R	A	N	X	O	O
C	A	D	D	R	E	S	S	E	S	N
S	B	A	J	O	U	R	N	E	Y	T

2 Complete the sentences with the words from Activity 1.

a Underground trains come out of their ...tunnels.... near Aldgate.

b When trains go over points, they change ....

c Someone heard a .... on the railway line.

d Cadogan had no ticket for his .... on the underground.

e Perhaps Cadogan fell from the .... of a train.

f There was no .... under Cadogan's body when Mason found it.

g Do they know the time of Cadogan's .... ?

h Holmes asks Mycroft for the names and .... of all the foreign agents in London.

i Holmes and Watson want to take a .... from Woolwich Station.

GUESS WHAT

What happens in the next chapter? Tick one picture.

a Holmes talks to Sir James Walter.

b Violet Cadogan comes to Baker Street.

c Holmes and Watson meet Sir James Walter's brother.

d Sidney Johnson shows Holmes the safe at Woolwich Arsenal.

3. A Second Death

We soon arrived at Sir James Walter's house by the river. The weather was better now, and the sun came out.

A **butler** opened the door to us.

'Can I help you?' he asked.

'We'd like to see Sir James Walter,' said Holmes. 'I'm Sherlock Holmes and this is Dr Watson.'

The butler's face went white.

'I'm sorry,' he said, 'But Sir James is dead. He died this morning.'

'Dead!' cried Holmes. 'How?'

The butler looked at us with his tired eyes.

'Please come in,' he said. 'You must speak to Sir James's brother, Colonel Valentine Walter.'

We took off our hats, and went into the sitting room. Minutes later, a tall man in a black suit came in and sat down. He was about fifty years old, **nervous**, and he spoke very quickly.

'My brother was a good man,' he began. 'When the plans **disappeared**, he felt very bad. He felt responsible, you see, because he had the key to the safe. When this happened, he didn't want to live any more. He broke down and died.'

'I'm very sorry,' I said.

'We wanted to speak to your brother,' said Holmes, 'because the most important plans are now missing, and we need to find them.'

butler the most important servant in a house

nervous feeling a little afraid, or badly excited about something

disappear to go away suddenly

'But why did Cadogan do this?' asked Colonel Walter. 'And how did he take the plans from the safe at Woolwich Arsenal? My brother couldn't understand it.'

'And you know nothing about it?' asked Holmes.

'Nothing,' answered the colonel. 'Now, excuse me, but I have many things to do.'

'Of course,' I said.

Holmes gave Colonel Walter a long look before we left.

In the street, Holmes said, 'The colonel is not a happy man, Watson.'

'Of course not!' I said. 'His brother died this morning.'

'That's true. But he didn't tell us everything, I feel.'

Next we went to visit Violet Cadogan. We found her at home in a little house with a nice front garden.

'I can't understand it,' she told us in her sitting room. 'Arthur loved his country.'

'Did he need money?' asked Holmes.

'No,' answered Violet. 'The government **paid** him well.'

'Then was he **worried** about something?' asked Holmes.

Violet said nothing for some minutes, but when she spoke, Holmes listened very carefully.

'Yes, he was worried about something in the last week of his **life**,' she said, 'I asked him about it, and he told me: he was worried about something at work.'

pay *(past* **paid***)* to give money to someone for something

worried not happy about something and thinking a lot about it

life what you live

'Did he say any more?' Holmes asked.

'He talked about foreign agents. They were interested in some plans, he said, but I didn't listen very carefully.'

'So he was worried in the last week of his life, but not before?' said Holmes.

'That's right,' answered Violet.

'And what happened on Monday evening?'

'Well, we had tickets for the theatre. We left the house at about seven o'clock in the **fog**. We were in a street near Woolwich Arsenal when Arthur suddenly ran away.'

'Why?' asked Holmes.

'I don't know,' she answered. 'He didn't say a thing. He disappeared into the fog, and I never saw him again. I walked home. On Tuesday morning, someone from Woolwich Arsenal came and asked about Arthur because he wasn't at work. Then, at twelve o'clock, I heard the **news**: Arthur was dead.'

Holmes looked at me worriedly.

'Arthur wasn't a **thief**,' Violet told us. 'He was a good man.'

'Yes, well, thank you for your help, Mrs Cadogan,' said Holmes. 'And now we must go.'

We left the house, and took a cab to Woolwich Arsenal.

'Now let's talk to Mr Sidney Johnson,' said Holmes.

Johnson met us at the Woolwich Arsenal office. He was a tall man with **glasses**, and he was about forty years old.

'Did you hear about Sir James?' he asked nervously.

'Yes. We spoke to his brother this morning,' I answered.

'First Cadogan dies, and now Sir James! What is happening? And why did Cadogan take those plans?'

fog bad weather that makes it not very easy to see

news when someone tells you something that is new

thief (plural **thieves**) a person who takes things without asking

glasses you wear these in front of your eyes to help you see better

'So he took them, you think,' said Holmes. 'Why?'

'Well, I never thought badly of him before,' answered Johnson, 'but *I* didn't take those papers – and *Sir James* didn't take them. So that leaves Cadogan!'

'Right. And what time did you close the office on Monday?' asked Holmes.

'At five o'clock,' said Johnson. 'And the plans were in the safe when I left.'

'Hmm. So the thief needed three different keys for his work that evening. Am I right?'

'Yes,' Johnson answered. 'The key to Woolwich Arsenal, the key to this office, and the key to the safe.'

'But Cadogan didn't have any of those keys, and the police found no keys on his body. So how did he take the plans?' asked Holmes.

'I don't know,' said Johnson. 'My keys were with *me*, and Sir James took *his* keys to London when he left.'

'Right. Now, only seven of the ten papers were in Cadogan's pockets,' said Holmes. 'Three papers are missing. Can someone make the submarine with those three papers?'

'No,' Johnson answered. 'They need all ten of them, I think.'

'But the missing papers are the most important,' said Holmes.

'They are,' said Johnson.

'Then we must move fast!' said Holmes. 'Come, Watson.'

READING CHECK

Are these sentences true or false?

		True	False
a	Sherlock Holmes is a famous detective.	☑	☐
b	Sir James Walter's house is by the river.	☐	☐
c	Colonel Valentine Walter tells Holmes and Watson about his brother's death.	☐	☐
d	Violet talks about the Cadogans' evening at the theatre.	☐	☐
e	Holmes and Watson take a cab to Woolwich Arsenal.	☐	☐
f	The thief needed three different keys to take the plans.	☐	☐
g	Three of the ten papers were in Cadogan's pockets.	☐	☐

WORD WORK

1 Correct the underlined words in these sentences. They are all new words in Chapter 3.

a When the plans <u>disapproved</u>, Sir James felt responsible. …disappeared…

b Cadogan walked away in the <u>dog</u>, and Violet never saw him again. ………………………

c Did the government <u>day</u> Cadogan well? ………………………

d Cadogan didn't have a long <u>like</u>. He died young. ………………………

e Did you hear the latest <u>noise</u> about the top-secret plans? ………………………

2 The bold letters in each sentence come from a new word in Chapter 3. Complete each word with the letters in brackets at the end of the sentence.

a I work for Sir James Walter. I'm his **b u t l e r**. (**etu**)

b When Colonel Walter spoke to Holmes, he was **n _ _ v _ _ s**. (**reuo**)

c Not long before he died, Cadogan was very **w _ _ r _ _ d**. (**roei**)

d Johnson is tall, and he wears **g _ a _ _ _ s**. (**sels**)

e Who were the top-secret plan **t _ _ ev _ s**? (**ehi**)

GUESS WHAT

What happens in the next chapter? Tick the boxes.

a At Woolwich Arsenal, Holmes and Watson go
  1 into the garden. ☐
  2 up on the roof. ☐
  3 over the river. ☐

b At Woolwich Station, Holmes and Watson speak to
  1 Violet Cadogan. ☐
  2 a ticket office worker. ☐
  3 a foreign agent. ☐

c Back at Baker Street, Holmes finds
  1 a letter from Mycroft. ☐
  2 a letter from Colonel Walter. ☐
  3 a telegram from Lestrade. ☐

d Holmes wants to go to the house of a foreign agent with
  1 Lestrade. ☐
  2 Mycroft. ☐
  3 Watson. ☐

Royal Arsenal, Woolwich

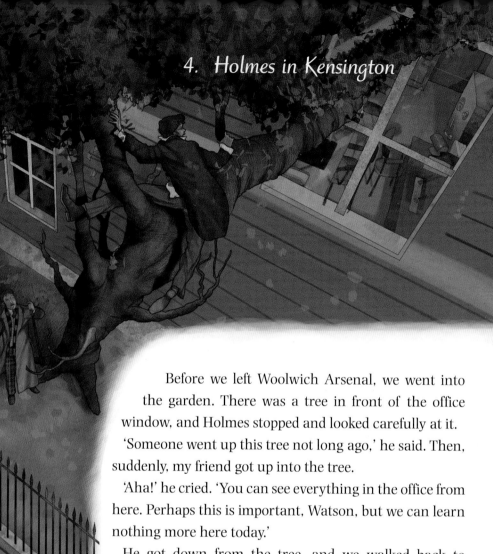

4. Holmes in Kensington

Before we left Woolwich Arsenal, we went into the garden. There was a tree in front of the office window, and Holmes stopped and looked carefully at it.

'Someone went up this tree not long ago,' he said. Then, suddenly, my friend got up into the tree.

'Aha!' he cried. 'You can see everything in the office from here. Perhaps this is important, Watson, but we can learn nothing more here today.'

He got down from the tree, and we walked back to Woolwich Station. At the ticket office, we spoke to a young ticket office worker.

'I saw Mr Cadogan on Monday evening,' he told us. 'He came here at about eight o'clock, and I sold him a ticket to London. He was very nervous when he asked for it. He took the 8.15 train to London Bridge.'

We thanked the man, and took a train back to London. Holmes said nothing on our journey.

Back in London, he asked me, 'So what did we learn in Woolwich, Watson? Let's think. Cadogan was worried in the last week of his life, and very nervous on Monday evening. Why? Perhaps a foreign agent wanted the Bruce-Partington plans, but Cadogan didn't want to help him. He left home with his wife on Monday evening for the theatre. He had two theatre tickets in his pocket, so why did he disappear? Why did he run away, and leave Violet in the street? Perhaps he saw the foreign agent again in the fog that night. Cadogan followed the man, and saw him take the papers from the safe at Woolwich Arsenal – perhaps from the tree by the window.'

'But he didn't call for help,' I said. 'Why was that?'

'A good question, Watson,' answered Holmes. 'Perhaps the thief wasn't a foreign agent, but someone important from Woolwich Arsenal. Perhaps the important man **escaped**, and Cadogan took a train to London because he knew his address. What happened next? I don't know. But some hours later, Mason found Cadogan's dead body on the underground railway line near Aldgate Station.'

Back at Baker Street, we found a **message** from Mycroft. It gave the names and addresses of the important foreign agents in London at the time:

Holmes,
I have three names for you:
– **Wolfgang Meyer**, 13 Great George Street, Westminster
– **Louis La Rothière**, Campden Mansions, Notting Hill
– **Hugo Oberstein**, 13 Caulfield Gardens, Kensington
Oberstein was in London on Monday, but he left the next day. The government is very worried.

Mycroft

escape to run away from something

message you write this to someone

Wolfgang Meyer /ˌwɒlfgæŋ ˈmeɪə/

Louis La Rothiere /ˌluːɪ læ ˈrɒtjeə/

Hugo Oberstein /ˌhjuːgəʊ ˈəʊbəstaɪn/

map a picture that shows where streets and railway lines are in a town

crowbar a metal stick that someone uses to break open a door or window

lamp a thing that helps you to see in the dark

chisel a tool for cutting, shaping, or marking wood, stone, or metal

Holmes looked at his big **map** of London, and found the three addresses on it.

'Good!' he said, and smiled. 'I must go out now, Watson. Please wait here.'

I waited three long hours. At about nine o'clock, a boy arrived with a message from Holmes:

> Watson,
>
> I'm having dinner at Goldini's Italian Restaurant in Kensington. Please come at once. And bring a **crowbar**, a **lamp**, and a **chisel**.
>
> S. H.

I took a cab to the restaurant, and found Holmes at a table by the window. I sat down with him.

'Do you have everything with you?' he asked.

'Yes,' I answered. 'And nobody in the street saw me with it because it's all under my coat.'

'Very good, Watson. Now listen. Cadogan's body didn't fall out of a train but from the roof of a train. This happened when it went over the points at Aldgate and changed direction. So someone put his body on that train roof. But how?'

I couldn't answer.

'Tell me, Holmes,' I said.

'Very well. In West London, some of the underground railway lines leave their tunnels and are open to the sky. The back windows of different houses **overlook** these open railway lines. When a train stops under one of these windows, a man – or perhaps two men – can put a body on the roof of it. Trains often stop and wait under the back window of a house here in Kensington. The address is 13 Caulfield Gardens. It's the home of a foreign agent, Mr Hugo Oberstein – and he left London on Tuesday!'

'Ah, so you left me at Baker Street for this!' I cried.

'Yes, Watson. Earlier this evening I went and looked at the railway line behind 13 Caulfield Gardens. A train stopped there when I arrived – under Oberstein's back window! Oberstein put Cadogan's body on the roof of a train through that window!'

'But where is Oberstein now?' I asked. 'We need to find him, and the Bruce-Partington plans!'

'Oberstein is in Paris,' Holmes answered. 'He wants to sell the plans there – and he's asking a lot of money for them!'

'So what can we do?' I asked.

'We can **break into** his house,' said Holmes. 'There's nobody there now, but perhaps there's something interesting in the house. Remember: we know Oberstein killed Cadogan and took the plans. But Oberstein doesn't know about us.'

'But do we need to break into his house?' I asked. 'Let's talk to Lestrade about this.'

'There's no time, Watson,' said Holmes. 'You can wait in the street, but I must get into Oberstein's house tonight.'

We got up, Holmes paid, and then we left the restaurant.

'Let's walk there,' said Holmes. 'It's not far. This is going to be a very interesting visit, I think!'

overlook to look out on something (of a window)

break into (past **broke into**) to go into a place by breaking the door or window

READING CHECK

Correct nine more mistakes in this summary of chapter 4.

In the garden at Woolwich Arsenal, Sherlock Holmes finds a ~~safe~~ *tree*. From here, he can see nothing in the office. Someone went up the tree not long after. Holmes and Watson drive back to Woolwich. At the theatre, they speak to a ticket office worker. Back at Baker Street, they find a message from Lestrade, with the names and addresses of all the foreign agents in England. Holmes goes out, and later Watson meets him at an Indian restaurant in Kensington. Watson brings some things with him in his hat. Holmes wants to visit Cadogan's house that night.

WORD WORK

1 Look at the pictures, and complete the crossword on page 25.

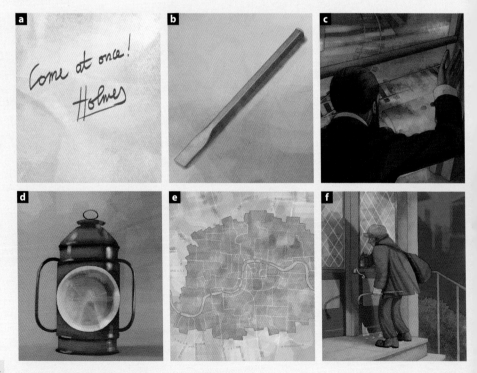

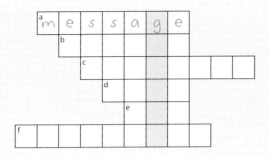

	a	m	e	s	s	a	g	e	
		b							
			c						
				d					
					e				
	f								

2 Which language does Oberstein usually speak? Read the blue squares down, and write the language here:

. . . .

GUESS WHAT

What happens in the next chapter? Tick the boxes.

		Yes	No
a	Holmes breaks into Oberstein's house that night.	☐	☐
b	Holmes has a fight with Oberstein, but he escapes.	☐	☐
c	Holmes and Watson find Cadogan's blood in the house.	☐	☐
d	Holmes and Watson find the missing plans in the house.	☐	☐
e	Holmes tells Mycroft and Lestrade about the house in Kensington.	☐	☐
f	Holmes and Watson go back to the house with Mycroft and Lestrade.	☐	☐

5. Messages from Pierrot

We soon arrived at Caulfield Gardens. The houses there were all very big. Holmes brought me to number 13, and we looked at the front door. It was big and **heavy**.

'We can never break in here, Holmes,' I said.

'You're right,' he answered. 'People in the street can see us very easily here. And any of them can call the police in a minute. Let's go down to the **basement**.'

We soon stood by the basement door. 'I don't like this, Holmes,' I said. 'We always work with the police.'

'Look, we're doing this for our country,' answered Holmes coldly. 'Now give me the crowbar.'

Holmes was right, I knew. We had important work that night. I took the crowbar from under my coat and gave it to him. I didn't watch him open the door. I looked up at the street, but saw no police.

The door was soon open, and we went into the house. I closed the door behind us, and we went upstairs. Holmes stopped at a window.

'Watson, this is it!' he cried. He opened the window, and we looked down at the railway line in front of it.

'Was I right?' Holmes asked me.

'Yes, Holmes,' I said. 'You're always right.'

'Not always, Watson, but look: they put the body here before they put it on the roof of the train. There's blood on the window – Cadogan's blood!'

It was true. I could see the blood on the window.

'Let's stay here for a minute or two,' said Holmes.

We didn't need to wait long. A train arrived and stopped under our window. It was easy to put a body on the roof from here, I could see.

heavy not easy to move, or to carry

basement downstairs from the ground floor of a house

26

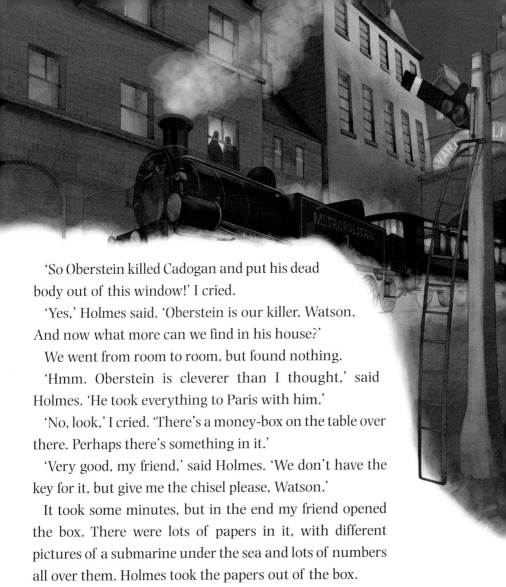

'So Oberstein killed Cadogan and put his dead
body out of this window!' I cried.

'Yes,' Holmes said. 'Oberstein is our killer, Watson.
And now what more can we find in his house?'

We went from room to room, but found nothing.

'Hmm. Oberstein is cleverer than I thought,' said
Holmes. 'He took everything to Paris with him.'

'No, look,' I cried. 'There's a money-box on the table over
there. Perhaps there's something in it.'

'Very good, my friend,' said Holmes. 'We don't have the
key for it, but give me the chisel please, Watson.'

It took some minutes, but in the end my friend opened
the box. There were lots of papers in it, with different
pictures of a submarine under the sea and lots of numbers
all over them. Holmes took the papers out of the box.

'How can these help us?' I said.

'They can't,' Holmes answered. 'But what's this?'

There was an **envelope** in the box, too. Holmes took this
out, and opened it. There were four messages in it.

'These are from a newspaper,' said Holmes. 'Someone
put these messages in *The Times*, I think. Look, Watson,
here's the first one, and this is the second.'

envelope a
paper cover that
you put on a letter

Pierrot
/ˈpjeərəʊ/

knock to hit with
your hand

Holmes put the messages on the table, and I read them:

Would like to hear from you soon. Happy to pay.
Write to me at my address. – **PIERROT**

Must have all papers. Bring them at once. Can pay
you then. – PIERROT

Need papers now. Write to me. Then wait for my
message in newspaper. – PIERROT

Monday night at nine o'clock. Come to my house.
Knock three times on door. Happy to pay when I
have papers. – PIERROT

'*Pierrot*, of course, is Oberstein,' I said.

'Yes, Watson,' Holmes answered. 'But who read these messages? And who came here at nine o'clock on Monday night? Perhaps this man took the top-secret plans from Woolwich! Let's go. We can't do any more here tonight.'

We left the house quietly, and soon found a cab.

'To the offices of *The Times*,' Holmes told the driver.

'Why there, Holmes?' I asked.

My friend smiled.

'*Pierrot* is going to put a fifth message in tomorrow's newspaper, I think,' he said.

We were not at the newspaper offices for long. Soon I was back at Baker Street, and in bed. I felt very tired.

The next morning, Holmes and I ate breakfast early. Mycroft and Lestrade arrived at half past eight.

'Good morning, Mycroft,' said Sherlock. 'Good morning, Lestrade. Please sit down.'

Then he told them about our visit to Caulfield Gardens.

'So you broke into the house, Mr Holmes!' said Lestrade. He wasn't very happy.

'Yes, we did, Lestrade. I'm sorry. But we did it for Britain!' Holmes answered.

'Well, the police do things differently,' said Lestrade. 'You must be careful, Mr Holmes.'

'Oh, we were very careful,' said Holmes. 'What do you think, Mycroft?'

'Very good, Sherlock,' Mycroft answered with a big smile. 'But what now?'

Holmes gave *The Times* to his brother. 'Today's newspaper has a new message from *Pierrot* – or Sherlock Holmes – in it,' he said.

Mycroft read it to us:

> Tonight. **Same** time, same address. Knock three times. Very important. – PIERROT

same not different

'Good. So we're going to Caulfield Gardens tonight. But who's going to visit us there?' asked Lestrade.

'Let's wait and see,' answered Holmes.

At eight o'clock that evening, Holmes and I took a cab to Kensington. We met Mycroft and Lestrade near Caulfield Gardens. We broke into Oberstein's house again, and waited. At nine o'clock, we heard three knocks on the heavy front door.

29

READING CHECK

What do they say? Complete the sentences with the words from the speech bubbles.

1 We're doing this for our country.

2 To the offices of *The Times*.

3 We can never break in here.

4 Oberstein is cleverer than I thought.

5 Tonight. Same time, same address.

6 So you broke into the house!

a Watson tells Holmes at Obsertein's front door,
' We can never break in here. '

b Holmes says to Watson coldly,
' '

c When they find nothing important in the house, Holmes tells Watson,
' '

d Holmes says to the cab driver,
' '

e When Lestrade learns of Holmes's visit to Caulfield Gardens, he says,
' '

f Mycroft reads from the newspaper,
' '

ACTIVITIES

WORD WORK

Complete each sentence with a word in the money box.

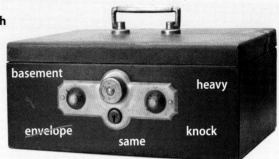

basement
heavy
envelope
same
knock

a Holmes found some old messages from 'Pierrot' in an ..envelope....

b Oberstein's front door was .... So Holmes and Watson couldn't break in there.

c In the end, they went into Oberstein's house through the .... door.

d Holmes put the .... name – *Pierrot* – on his new message in *The Times*.

e At nine o'clock, there was a .... at Oberstein's front door.

GUESS WHAT

How does the story finish? Tick three boxes.

a Colonel Walter goes to France. ☐

b Hugo Oberstein comes back to London. ☐

c Mycroft finds the top-secret plans in a French hotel. ☐

d Holmes and Watson go to Paris. ☐

e The top-secret plans come back to England. ☐

f The Queen thanks Sherlock Holmes for his good work. ☐

Holmes went downstairs in the dark, and opened the door.

'Come in,' he said. We heard someone come upstairs with him. When they were in the sitting room, Holmes quietly closed the door behind them. I **lit** the lamp.

The man saw us, pushed past Holmes, and began to run away across the room. Suddenly he fell over something, and hit his head on the door. He gave a cry, closed his eyes at once, and fell back at our feet.

'Sherlock, who is this?' asked Mycroft.

'Colonel Valentine Walter, Sir James's brother,' answered Sherlock. 'You see, Watson, the colonel didn't tell us everything! I felt it. Do you remember?'

'I do,' I answered, 'And you were right.'

light (*past* **lit**)
to give fire to
something

I helped Lestrade to put Colonel Walter on a chair. After some minutes, he opened his eyes.

He looked nervously at us all. 'What's happening?' he asked worriedly. 'I wanted to see Mr Oberstein.'

'Or *Pierrot*, perhaps!' said Holmes. 'Colonel Walter, we know everything. You took the Bruce-Partington plans. You wanted to sell them, and Arthur Cadogan died here!'

The colonel said nothing.

'Tell us your story,' said Holmes. 'Perhaps it can help.'

The colonel put his head in his hands, but didn't speak.

'Then I'm going to tell the story,' said Holmes. 'You needed money quickly because you had money **troubles**. So you made **copies** of your brother's keys – to Woolwich Arsenal, to the office, and to the safe.

'You wrote to Oberstein, and he put messages in *The Times* for you. On Monday night, you went to Woolwich Arsenal in the fog. You wanted to take the plans from the safe, but Cadogan saw you in the street and came after you. Perhaps he knew something of your money troubles. At Woolwich Arsenal, he watched you open the safe from a tree in front of the office. You took the papers, left Woolwich, and took a train to London. Cadogan went after you, and took the same train. In London, you walked to Kensington – or perhaps you took a cab – and you came to this address: 13 Caulfield Gardens. When Cadogan arrived some minutes later, you killed him!'

'No!' cried Walter. 'I'm not a killer. I took the papers from the safe, it's true, and I came here with them on Monday night, but I didn't kill Cadogan.'

'Then what happened?' asked Holmes. 'How did he die before you put his dead body on the roof of a train?'

troubles bad times when things are not easy

copy *(plural* **copies***)* when you make a second thing just like something; to write or draw something again

33

stick a long, thin piece of wood

detailed with lots of small and careful pieces of information

Colonel Walter was now happy to tell us everything:

*Yes, I had money troubles, and Cadogan knew about them. You were right there, Mr Holmes. I came here to Caulfield Gardens, and I knocked three times on the front door. When Oberstein opened the door, Cadogan arrived. He was very angry. He understood everything. He came into the house after me, and Oberstein suddenly hit him over the head with a big, heavy **stick**. Cadogan fell at our feet, dead. But what could we do with the body? We didn't know.*

Then Oberstein remembered something. 'Trains often stop on the railway line under my back window. So let's put the body on the roof of a train,' he said. 'But first I want to see those top-secret plans from Woolwich Arsenal. Give them to me!'

I gave him the papers. He looked through them, and said, 'I need to take these three papers from you.'

'You can't,' I answered. 'You must copy them. Then I can take all ten papers back to Woolwich and put them in the safe again. Nobody must know of this.'

*Oberstein said, 'Look, I can't copy these three papers because they're very **detailed**.'*

34

'Then I must take them with me tonight,' I told him.

Oberstein thought for a minute, and said, 'No. I'm going to keep these three papers, and we're going to put those seven papers in this young man's pocket. When the police find the plans on his body, he's going to be the thief in their eyes!'

I wasn't happy about this, but I said 'yes' to it. What could I do? We waited for half an hour at the window before a train stopped. We quickly put Cadogan on the roof of it. There was a lot of fog, so nobody saw us. Then I left this house, and went home to Woolwich. I never saw Oberstein again.'

Holmes looked at Colonel Walter coldly.

'And what about your brother – Sir James Walter?' he asked.

The colonel's eyes were suddenly old and tired.

'He saw me with his keys once, some weeks ago, and he knew about my money troubles. With my copies of his keys, I went and took those plans for Oberstein. Did my brother know about that, too? Perhaps. But he never spoke to me about it. James was a very good man, Mr Holmes, and this broke him. He died soon after.'

Nobody spoke for some minutes.

Then Mycroft said, 'Colonel Walter, you must help us. We need to find Oberstein. Where is he? Do you know?'

'In France,' answered the colonel. 'I have the address of a hotel in Paris. Oberstein gave it to me before he left. I could write to him there when I needed, he said.'

'Then you must write to him now,' said Holmes, 'and he must come back to London. Are you going to help us?'

'I am,' answered Colonel Walter. 'I didn't plan Cadogan's death, you know. I needed money badly – that was all!'

'Then take this pen and write,' said Holmes. He gave a

pen and paper to the colonel, and began to speak:

'Oberstein, my friend, you need a fourth paper, you know. I now have a copy of it, and I want more money from you for this. I cannot come to France because people are watching me, so please bring the money to the Charing Cross Hotel in London at eleven o'clock on Saturday morning. I can give you the fourth paper then.'

'Very clever, Mr Holmes,' said Lestrade. 'On Saturday morning we're going to get our man.'

For once, Lestrade was right. Oberstein came back to London after he read Colonel Walter's letter. He arrived at the Charing Cross Hotel on Saturday morning. The colonel wasn't there, but Lestrade and three big, young men from the London Police were. Oberstein couldn't escape. Lestrade **arrested** him, and he found all three of the missing papers in his bag. Soon after that, Oberstein went to **prison**. He stayed there for fifteen years, and when he came out of prison, he left Britain, and never came back.

Colonel Walter went to prison, too, and he died there six months later. He felt responsible for Cadogan's death, and

arrest to take a person to prison

prison a place where people must stay when they do something wrong

for his brother's death, too. And he couldn't live with that.

Mycroft thanked Sherlock and me for our work. Then he disappeared from our lives again for a very long time.

The next year, on a beautiful spring morning, Sherlock Holmes went to Buckingham **Palace**, and met the **Queen** there. She thanked him for his clever detective work, and they spoke for some time. Before Holmes left the palace, the Queen gave him a beautiful **tie-pin**. So when he wears that tie-pin now, perhaps he thinks back to the dark autumn of 1895 and our work for Mycroft and the British government. How could he forget the top-secret Bruce-Partington submarine plans, and their journey out of Britain for a time before they came back home again?

palace a big house where a queen lives

queen the most important woman in a country

tie-pin you fix a tie in place round your neck with this metal pin

READING CHECK

Correct the mistakes in the sentences.

Colonel Walter

a ~~Hugo Oberstein~~ comes upstairs after Holmes.

b The colonel wanted to see Holmes at the house.

c In the end, the colonel tells Holmes nothing about Cadogan's death.

d Cadogan came after the butler when he took the plans from Woolwich Arsenal.

e Because he needed money badly, the colonel wanted to sell the plans to Johnson.

f Oberstein killed Cadogan, and put his body through a back window onto a cab.

g The colonel writes to Oberstein in Germany with news of new paper for him.

h Lestrade goes to Charing Cross, and arrests Oberstein in the station there.

i Oberstein stays in prison for fifteen months.

j Colonel Walter goes to hospital, and he dies there after six weeks.

WORD WORK

Make words from the letters in the submarines to complete the sentences.

a When Watson .....lights..... the lamp, Colonel Walter sees Holmes, Watson, Mycroft, and Lestrade. ▸ **glthsi**

b The colonel had very bad money .... ▸ **storbuel**

c At Caulfield Gardens, Oberstein hit Cadogan on the head with a very heavy .... ▸ **kisct**

d At first, Obsertein wanted to .... all the top-secret plans. ▸ **pyoc**

e But three of the papers were very ...., and he could not do that with them. ▸ **talideed**

f After Lestrade .... Oberstein, he finds the missing papers. ▸ **sresrat**

g When Oberstein leaves ...., he goes away from Britain, and never comes back. ▸ **snorpi**

h Sherlock Holmes goes to Buckingham .... one spring morning. ▸ **elcapa**

i The .... is very happy with Holmes's work, and she wants to say 'thank you' to him. ▸ **eqenu**

j She gives a beautiful .... to the famous detective. ▸ **ite-nip**

GUESS WHAT

What happens after the story finishes? Tick your favourite sentences, and add ideas of your own.

a After they finish the Bruce-Partington submarine, Holmes goes and sees it. ☐

b The British government gives money to Violet Cadogan. ☐

c Violet marries again. ☐

c Oberstein meets Holmes when Holmes visits Germany. ☐

d The Queen goes on a journey under the sea in her new submarine. ☐

e Mycroft Holmes writes a book about his life. ☐

f Dr Watson leaves England and goes to India. ☐

g ....

h ....

i ....

j ....

39

Project A *Underground railways*

1 Read about the London Underground. Complete the information table below.

The London Underground opened in 1863 after the Metropolitan Railway Company built the first line. It is the oldest underground railway in the world.

The first line ran from Paddington to Farringdon. It carried 38,000 people on its first day. More lines opened between 1868 and 1904. Today London has eleven underground lines, and these run for over 400 kilometres. More than 1.2 billion people take the underground every year and there are 270 stations! The longest tunnel is nearly 28 kilometres long, but 55% of the London Underground is overground, and open to the sky. Hampstead Station in North London is the deepest London Underground station. It is 58 metres under the ground!

Year of opening	
First line	
Number of lines	
Total length of lines	
Number of passengers in a year	
Number of stations	
Longest tunnel	
Percentage of railway overground	
Deepest station	

2 Use the information in the table to complete the text about the Paris Métro.

Year of opening	1900
First line	Grande Arche to Château de Vincennes
Number of lines	sixteen
Total length of lines	over 210 kilometres
Number of passengers in a year	over 1.475 billion
Number of stations	303
Longest tunnel	nearly 20 kilometres
Percentage of railway overground	8%
Deepest station	Abbesses (36m) in Montmartre

The Paris Métro opened in.................. after the French Metropolitan Railway Company built the first line. The first line ran from.................. to .... Eight more lines opened between 1900 and 1920. Today .... has.................. underground lines, and these run for over .... More than.................. people take the Métro every year and there are.................. stations! The longest tunnel is nearly.................. long, but.................. of the Paris Métro is overground, and open to the sky. .... Station in.................. is the deepest Paris Métro station. It is.................. metres under the ground!

3 Write about the underground railway in a different city. Use the texts about the London Underground and Paris Métro to help you.

Berlin U-Bahn   **Moscow Metro**   **Tokyo Metro**

Buenos Aires Metro   **New York City Subway**

PROJECTS

Project B *Characters' thoughts*

1 Read this text. Tick a box to answer each question about it.

> Sherlock Holmes is a good detective. When he talks to people, he asks a lot of questions. Now he's asking Mason about the points on the railway line. Holmes is very excited about those points, but why? He doesn't want to tell me. I'm angry about that. Perhaps he's going to tell Dr Watson.

a Who is thinking this?
- ☐ Mycroft
- ☐ Dr Watson
- ☐ Lestrade

b Where does this happen?
- ☐ outside Aldgate Station
- ☐ at Woolwich Arsenal
- ☐ near Oberstein's house

c When does this happen?
- ☐ at night
- ☐ in the morning
- ☐ in the afternoon

2 Complete the different characters' thoughts from the scene in Sir James Walter's house with the words in the box.

| money | nervous | dead | back | government | troubles | arrest | plans | help |

Why did I take the plans? Now Cadogan's dead, and my brother's **a**).................., too. Sherlock Holmes knows everything. Last week I had money **b**).................., but now the police are going to **c**)................. me, and I'm going to go to prison. I'm afraid about that!

Colonel Walter didn't tell us everything when we last talked to him. I felt it. He was unhappy about Sir James's death, but I saw something more. He was **d**)................. and worried, too. Now we have him. He's going to **e**)................. us. And Oberstein is going to come **f**) .... to London with the top-secret plans. I'm excited about that!

My brother's very clever. I'm pleased with him. And the British **g**)................. are going to be very happy. Cadogan didn't take the **h**)................. . Sherlock knew that all along. Colonel Walter took them because he needed **i**)................. . I can see that now. But the colonel isn't a killer. I can see that, too.

3 Choose another scene from the story. Write the page number(s) the scene comes from here: ....

4 Choose one of the characters in that scene. Write notes about them in the table.

Character in the scene	What can he /she see and hear?	What is he / she thinking about?	How does he / she feel?

5 Write 40 – 50 words about the scene from your character's point of view.

6 Work in pairs. Read your character's thoughts aloud to your partner. Can he / she guess the story scene and the character?

GRAMMAR CHECK

Present Simple and Present Continuous

We use the Present Simple for things that are true in general, or things that happen regularly. *Watson lives in London. He usually reads The Times.*

We use the Present Continuous to talk about things happening now. We make it with be + the –ing form of the verb. *Holmes is opening a telegram in front of Watson.*

We make the –ing form by adding –ing to the infinitive without *to*. When a verb ends in –e, we remove the e and add –ing. *write – writing   live – living*

When short verbs end in consonant + vowel + consonant, we double the final consonant and add –ing. *hit – hitting*

1 Look at the picture. Complete the text with the verbs in brackets. Use the Present Simple or Present Continuous.

Sherlock Holmes **a)** .... lives ...... (live) with his friend
Dr Watson at a house in Baker Street. Usually they
b) .... (drink) coffee in the morning, but
today Lestrade and Mycroft Holmes **c)** ....
(visit). They **d)** .... (sit) on in the sitting room.
Sherlock Holmes **e)** .... (look) at his brother,
and he **f)** .... (listen) to him carefully.
Mycroft never usually **g)** .... (come) to
221B Baker Street!

2 Put the words in order. Write Present Simple or Present Continuous sentences.

a Mycroft's/at/is/Holmes/laughing/telegram
..Holmes is laughing at Mycroft's telegram...

b Mycroft/for/the/works/government/British
....

c Lestrade/telling/something/us/is/new
....

d about/plans/they/the/know/all
....

e out/Holmes/going/are/and I
....

45

Past Simple: information questions

In Past Simple questions, most verbs take did + subject + infinitive without *to*.

How did Watson know his name? From a newspaper story.

Where did Mason find the body? Near Aldgate Station.

With the verb *be*, we put the subject after the verb to make Past Simple questions.

Why were the papers in his pocket? Someone put them there.

Different question words before *did* or *be* ask for different information: how (= the way), where (= the place), why (= the reason), what (= the thing), who (= the person).

3 Holmes is beginning to think about Cadogan's death. Write correct question words and *did*, *was* or *were* in his questions.

a ...How did...Cadogan get on the train without a ticket?
We don't know.

b ....Cadogan's body near Aldgate Station?
Perhaps it fell from a train.

c ....the papers in Cadogan's pocket?
The top-secret submarine plans.

d ....Cadogan go to London that night?
Perhaps he saw someone with the plans.

e ....Cadogan see in the fog?
Perhaps he saw someone from Woolwich Arsenal.

f ....Cadogan's body fall from the roof of a train?
When the train went over the points, and it changed direction.

g ....someone take the papers from the safe at Woolwich Arsenal?
They had keys to the safe, the office, and the Arsenal.

h ....it say in the newspaper?
There were some papers in Cadogan's pocket.

GRAMMAR CHECK

Going to future: affirmative and negative

We make the going to future with the verb to be + going to + infinitive without *to*.
We use the *going to* future for plans, intensions and predictions.

Lestrade is going to come with us. (= plan)   *We're going to find the killer.* (= intention)

It isn't going to be easy. (= prediction)

4 Read Sherlock Holmes's notes. Write sentences about his plans.

> THINGS TO DO
> ~~Visit Aldgate Station.~~
> Speak to Violet Cadogan at home.
> Find Sir James Walter's house.
> Talk to Sidney Johnson at Woolwich Arsenal.
> Get names and addresses of all foreign agents in London.

a We're going to visit Aldgate Station.

b ....

c ....

d ....

e ....

5 Holmes tells Watson his predictions. Put his words in order, and make sentences using the *going to* future.

a isn't/Lestrade /about this/happy/be/going to

Lestrade isn't going to be happy about this.

b Oberstein's house/we're/learn more/going to/in

....

c my message/read/is/in the newspaper/going to/the thief

....

d everything/us/tell/Colonel Walter/going to/is

....

e the colonel's letter/answer/Oberstein/going to/is

....

GRAMMAR CHECK

Adjectives and adverbs of manner

We use adjectives to describe people or things.   *He was a young man.*   *It was a dark night.*

We use adverbs of manner to describe how people do things.   *Holmes spoke quickly.*

We make adverbs of manner from adjectives by adding –ly.   *nice – nicely*

For adjectives that end in –y. we change y to –ily.   *happy – happily*

6 **Use the adjective or adverb to complete the correct sentence in each pair.**

a **clever/cleverly**

  i) Sherlock Holmes ...cleverly... puts a message in *The Times* from *Pierrot*.

  ii) Sherlock's brother Mycroft is a very ....clever.... man.

b **quiet/quietly**

  i) Violet Cadogan spoke very ....

  ii) Oberstein's house was .... when Holmes and
    Watson arrived.

c **cold/coldly**

  i) Sherlock Holmes has ...., blue eyes.

  ii) 'We're doing this for our country,' said Holmes .... to Watson.

d **careful/carefully**

  i) Watson .... put the crowbar and lamp under his coat.

  ii) Lestrade is a very .... detective.

e **heavy/heavily**

  i) Cadogan's body fell .... from the roof of a train.

  ii) Oberstein's house had a thick, ... door.

f **angry/angrily**

  i) 'You broke into the house!' said Lestrade .... to Holmes.

  ii) Sir James Walter was .... when the thief took the plans from his office.

g **nervous/nervously**

  i) Watson felt .... when Holmes broke into Oberstein's house.

  ii) Sidney Johnson asked ...., 'Did you hear about Sir James?'

GRAMMAR CHECK

Modal auxiliary verbs: *can*, *can't*, *must*

We use can + infinitive without *to* to talk about things that we are able to do, or that are allowed.   *You can take a train to Woolwich.*

We use can't + infinitive without *to* to talk about things that we are not able to do, or that are not allowed.   *You can't get into Woolwich Arsenal without three keys.*

We use must + infinitive without *to* to talk about things that we think are necessary or very important, or that are an obligation.   *You must help us, Sherlock.*

7 Correct the mistakes in these sentences.

a Sherlock Holmes must to talk to Sidney Johnson.

b Cadogan can't opening the safe without a key.

c Watson cans see the railway line from Oberstein's window.

d 'We must doing this for our country, Watson,' says Holmes

e Lestrade tells Holmes: 'You don't can do this.'

8 Use *can*, *can't* or *must* to complete Lestrade's words to Sherlock Holmes.

a You …must… find the plans. They're very important.

b You …………… visit people when they're at home. That's OK.

c You …………… break into people's houses. That's wrong.

d You …………… be very careful. I'm worried for your life.

e You …………… tell me everything. I want to know it all.

f You …………… ask a lot of questions. That's all right.

g You …………… break down doors. It isn't right.

h You …………… find Cadogan's killer. I want to arrest him.

GRAMMAR CHECK

Past Simple *Yes/No* questions and short answers

We use was/were + the subject, or the auxiliary verbs did and could + infinitive without *to* in *Yes/No* questions in the Past Simple.

Was Oberstein at home when Sherlock Holmes broke in?

Did Violet Cadogan go to the theatre in the end?

We do not use question words in Yes/No questions. We are not interested in information but in a short answer – 'yes' or 'no'.

In the short answer, we re-use was/were or the auxiliary verb.

No, he wasn't = (was not). *No, she didn't.* (= did not)

9 **Write answers for Lestrade's questions to Oberstein. Use the short answers in the box.**

> No, he didn't.   Yes, he could.   ~~No, I didn't.~~   Yes, I was.
> Yes, I did.   Yes, he was.   Yes, I did.   No, I couldn't.

a Did you break into Woolwich Arsenal?

....No, I didn't....................

b Could Colonel Walter visit Woolwich Arsenal easily?

....

c Did Cadogan bring the plans to London?

....

d Did you put messages in *The Times* for Colonel Walter?

....

e Were you at Caulfield Gardens when Cadogan arrived?

....

f Did you kill Cadogan?

....

g Was Colonel Walter there when you killed Cadogan?

....

h Could you sell the top-secret plans in London?

....

GRAMMAR CHECK

Time clauses with *before*, *after*, and *when*

Before links a later action with an earlier main action.

Before he broke into Oberstein's house, <u>Holmes ate dinner at Goldini's</u>. (= earlier action)

After links an earlier action with a later main action.

<u>Holmes and Watson went to see Sidney Johnson</u> after they spoke to Violet Cadogan, (= later action)

When links two actions near in time. The 'when' action happens first.

Lestrade arrested Oberstein when he came back to London,

When we write the time clause first, we use a comma.

When Oberstein arrived at the hotel, Lestrade met him.

10 **Complete the newspaper story about the top-secret plans with *before*, *after* or *when*.**

QUEEN THANKS HOLMES

Yesterday Mr Sherlock Holmes, the famous detective, met the Queen at Buckingham Palace. She thanked him for his detective work, and **a)** ...before... he left the palace, she gave him a beautiful tie-pin.

What did Mr Holmes do? **b)** .... the government needed to find the top-secret Bruce-Partington submarine plans, he was happy to help. **c)** .... the plans disappeared from Woolwich Arsenal, London police found the dead body of an office worker, Arthur Cadogan, near Aldgate Station. Did he take the plans? 'No,' thought Holmes. **d)** .... he learnt the name of Cadogan's killer, he knew the answer at once. Hugo Oberstein, a foreign agent, had the plans. But Oberstein was in Paris! **e)** .... the police could arrest him, Holmes needed to bring Oberstein back to London.

Mr Holmes was very clever, and Oberstein came back with the plans. **f)** .... the police arrested him, he went to prison for a long time.

DOMINOES Your Choice

Read *Dominoes* for pleasure, or to develop language skills. It's your choice.

Each *Domino* reader includes:
- a good story to enjoy
- integrated activities to develop reading skills and increase vocabulary
- task-based projects – perfect for CEFR portfolios
- contextualized grammar activities

Each *Domino* pack contains a reader, and an excitingly dramatized audio recording of the story

If you liked this *Domino*, read these:

The Swiss Family Robinson
David Johann Wyss

'There's going to be a storm,' Father told Fritz. 'Find your brothers and bring them to our room.'
A Swiss family are going to Australia when their ship sinks in a storm. After that, Mother, Father, Fritz, Hans, Ernst, and little Franz must make their home on a Pacific Island. Like Robinson Crusoe, they have many exciting times on the island, and they learn a lot about its animals and plants. But do they always want to stay there, or are they going to leave one day?

Journey to the West
Retold by Janet Hardy Gould

'Tripitaka, can you go to the west for me – and for Buddha?'
When the holy woman Guanyin asks the young Chinese monk Tripitaka to bring some holy writings back from India, he says 'yes'. But how can he travel across rivers, and fight terrible monsters and demons, on his long journey? He needs three strong helpers – Monkey, Pigsy, and Sandy – to do that! But where do they come from? Do they always help? And can they bring the holy writings home again? Read this old Chinese story, and learn.

	CEFR	Cambridge Exams	IELTS	TOEFL iBT	TOEIC
Level 3	B1	PET	4.0	57-86	550
Level 2	A2–B1	KET-PET	3.0-4.0	–	390
Level 1	A1–A2	YLE Flyers/KET	3.0	–	225
Starter & Quick Starter	A1	YLE Movers	1.0–2.0	–	–

You can find details and a full list of books and teachers' resources on our website:
www.oup.com/elt/gradedreaders